Houghton
Mifflin
Harcourt

JOURNEYS
COMMON CORE

Program Authors

James F. Baumann · David J. Chard · Jamal Cooks
J. David Cooper · Russell Gersten · Marjorie Lipson
Lesley Mandel Morrow · John J. Pikulski · Héctor H. Rivera
Mabel Rivera · Shane Templeton · Sheila W. Valencia
Catherine Valentino · MaryEllen Vogt

Consulting Author

Irene Fountas

Unit 3

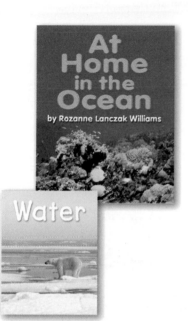
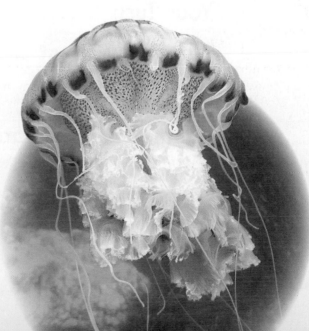

Welcome, Reader!

Each day you are becoming a better reader. Good for you!

The stories in this book will take you to the sea, the jungle, and the desert. You will see animals that are furry, scaly, slinky, feathered, striped, and spotted. You will even read about manatees!

Get ready to read new words, visit new places, and learn about the world around us!

Sincerely,

The Authors

Unit 3

At
Home
in the
Ocean
by Rozanne Lanczak Williams

Water

☑ **WORDS TO KNOW**
High-Frequency Words

cold

where

blue

live

far

their

little

water

Vocabulary Reader

Context Cards

Shark

COMMON CORE   **RF.1.3g** recognize and read irregularly spelled words

10   Go Digital

Words to Know

Read Together

▶ Read each Context Card.

▶ Make up a new sentence that uses a blue word.

1 **cold**

This ocean water is very cold.

2 **where**

Sharks live where the ocean is deep.

3 blue

Today the ocean water looks blue.

4 live

Whales live in all the oceans of the world.

5 far

Squid swim far below the ocean's surface.

6 their

Their home is by the ocean.

7 little

Many little fish live in the ocean.

8 water

Some people take photos in the water.

Read and Comprehend

Read Together

Go Digital

At Home in the Ocean
by Rozanne Lanczak Williams

☑ **TARGET SKILL**

Author's Purpose Authors may write to make you laugh or to give information. The reason an author writes is called the **author's purpose**. In informational texts, the author's purpose is to give information about a topic. As you read, think about what the author wants you to learn. List details that explain the author's purpose.

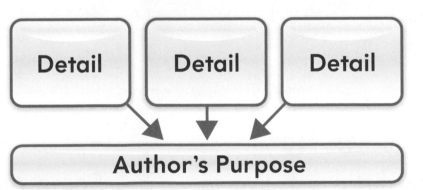

```
[ Detail ]   [ Detail ]   [ Detail ]
      \          |          /
       →         ↓         ←
         [ Author's Purpose ]
```

☑ **TARGET STRATEGY**

Analyze/Evaluate Tell what you think and how you feel about the selection. Tell why.

COMMON CORE

RI.1.8 identify the reasons an author gives to support points

Marine Habitats

Oceans are very big. They are filled with many kinds of plants and animals. Some animals live on the bottom of the ocean. Other animals, like whales, swim far in the water. They come to the top to breathe. Some fish live deep down under the water where it is cold and dark. Some of them can even light up!

You will read more about life in the ocean in **At Home in the Ocean**.

ANCHOR TEXT

At
Home
in the
Ocean
by Rozanne Lanczak Williams

✓ TARGET SKILL

Author's Purpose Find details the author uses to explain her purpose.

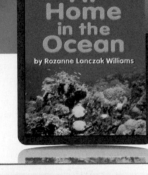

✓ GENRE

Informational text gives facts about a topic. Look for:
► information and facts in the words
► photos that show the real world
► labels for photos

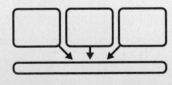

RI.1.2 identify the main topic and retell key details; **RI.1.8** identify the reasons an author gives to support points; **RI.1.10** read informational texts

Go Digital

Meet the Author
Rozanne Lanczak Williams

When Rozanne Lanczak Williams first became a teacher, she lived far from the ocean. She and her students learned a lot about sea life, though, from their research and by making beautiful underwater murals. Now Ms. Williams lives only seven miles from the ocean! To write this story, she hunted for fun fishy facts. She visited a big aquarium, the library, a bookstore, a friend's classroom library—and the ocean!

At Home in the Ocean

by Rozanne Lanczak Williams

ESSENTIAL QUESTION

What kinds of plants and animals would you find in the ocean?

15

The ocean is big!
It is big and blue as far as you can see.

It is home to many plants and animals.

The biggest animals in the ocean are blue whales. They eat little animals called krill.

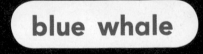

blue whale

krill

Many animals live in cold water.
Brrr!

penguins

Penguins swim fast! They flap their wings to zip, zip, zip in the water.

Manatees live where the water is warm.

They do not swim fast.

manatees

Manatees eat lots and lots of plants.
Then they rest.

This turtle swims far!

It digs in the sand and lays its eggs.

Then it swims back to its ocean home.

turtle

eggs

kelp

Kelp is the biggest plant in the ocean.
It can grow fast.

sea otter

Kelp can grow two feet in a day!
Sea otters can get lots of food here.

Lots of plants and animals, big and little, live in the ocean.
The ocean is their home.

Dig Deeper

How to Analyze the Text

Use these pages to learn about Author's Purpose and Details. Then read **At Home in the Ocean** again.

Author's Purpose

Authors write for many different reasons. Why do you think the author wrote **At Home in the Ocean**? What topic does she want you to learn about? You can find important details in the selection that help explain the author's topic. Use a chart to list the details and the author's purpose.

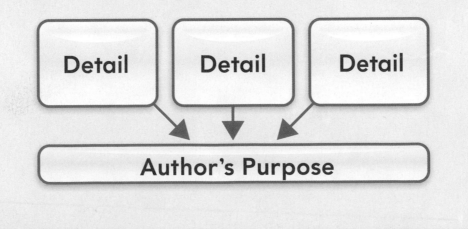

RI.1.2 identify the main topic and retell key details; **RI.1.8** identify the reasons an author gives to support points

Details

Details are facts and other bits of information. They tell more about a topic. A detail you learned in **At Home in the Ocean** is that manatees eat lots of plants.

What other details from this selection teach you about life in the ocean? You can find important details in the words and pictures.

Your Turn

RETURN TO THE ESSENTIAL QUESTION

 Turn and Talk

What kinds of plants and animals would you find in the ocean? Talk with a small group about what you learned. Use details from **At Home in the Ocean** to answer. Listen. Add your ideas to what others say.

💬 Classroom Conversation

Talk about these questions with your class.

1. Describe an animal or plant you learned about. Use details to tell more.

2. How are all the animals the same?

3. Which animal or plant would you like to learn more about? Why?

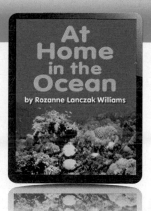

Response Write two facts that you learned from **At Home in the Ocean**. Find text evidence in the words and photos to get ideas. Use your own words when you write your facts.

Writing Tip

Add details that give more information about your topic.

Go Digital

COMMON CORE **RI.1.7** use illustrations and details to describe key ideas; **RI.1.8** identify the reasons an author gives to support points; **W.1.2** write informative/explanatory texts; **SL.1.1b** build on others' talk in conversations by responding to others' comments; **SL.1.4** describe people, places, things, and events with details/express ideas and feelings clearly

Read Together

Water

Informational text gives facts about a topic. This is from a science textbook.

A **diagram** is a drawing that can show how something works or the parts that make up something. What does the diagram on page 35 show?

COMMON CORE **RI.1.5** know and use text features to locate facts or information; **RI.1.10** read informational texts

Go Digital

Water

What is one thing that all living things, whether they are big or little, have in common? They need water to live.

Water comes in different forms. The water you drink is a liquid. A liquid flows and takes the shape of the container it is in.

ice

water

snow

Water can freeze into ice or snow. Frozen water is a solid. A solid has its own shape.

What is ice? Ice is water that has frozen. It is hard and cold.

Where does snow come from? Snow is tiny pieces of frozen water that fall from the clouds.

Ice and snow are found in many places around the world. The North Pole is one of these places. There is cold, blue water all around it. People cannot live that far north for very long, but some animals make their homes near the North Pole.

Compare Texts

At Home in the Ocean by Rozanne Lanczak Williams

Water

Read Together

TEXT TO TEXT

Compare Animals Use text evidence to compare the polar bear with an animal from **At Home in the Ocean**. How are they alike and different?

TEXT TO SELF

Describe It Find the photo of your favorite animal from either selection. How does it look? What does it do? Use the photo to help describe it.

TEXT TO WORLD

Use a Globe Use a globe to find two different oceans. Draw and label animals that you think might live in each ocean.

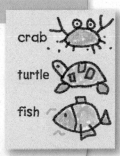

crab

turtle

fish

Go Digital

COMMON CORE **RI.1.3** describe the connection between individuals, events, ideas, or information in a text; **RI.1.7** use illustrations and details to describe key ideas; **RI.1.9** identify similarities in and differences between texts on the same topic; **SL.1.4** describe people, places, things, and events with details/express ideas and feelings clearly; **SL.1.5** add drawings or visual displays to descriptions to clarify ideas, thoughts, and feelings

Grammar

Proper Nouns A noun that names a special person, animal, place, or thing is called a **proper noun**. Proper nouns begin with capital letters.

When a **title** is used before a name, it begins with a capital letter, too. A title usually ends with a period.

Mr. Diaz   **Mrs.** Sims   **M**iss Reed

Try This!

Write each sentence on another sheet of paper. Find the proper nouns. Use capital letters and periods where they belong.

1. My family went to florida.

2. We drove on beach street.

3. We met mrs bell.

4. Her dog is named skippy.

5. I went on the super sun slide.

6. We all ate at snack shack.

 Grammar in Writing

When you proofread your writing, be sure you have used capital letters to write proper nouns.

Informative Writing

✓ **Sentence Fluency** Sometimes you will write **sentences** that give readers facts. One kind of fact describes how something happens.

Joy wrote about sea lions. Then she added **loudly** to describe how sea lions bark.

Revised Draft

> loudly
> A sea lion can bark. ∧

Writing Traits Checklist

✓ **Sentence Fluency** Do my sentences have words that tell **how**?

✓ Does my writing tell facts?

✓ Did I use capital letters correctly?

Look for words that tell **how** in Joy's final copy. Look for facts. Then revise your writing. Use the Checklist.

Final Copy

Sea Lions

Sea lions do amazing things. A sea lion can bark loudly. It uses its flippers to move quickly on land or in water.

Lesson 12

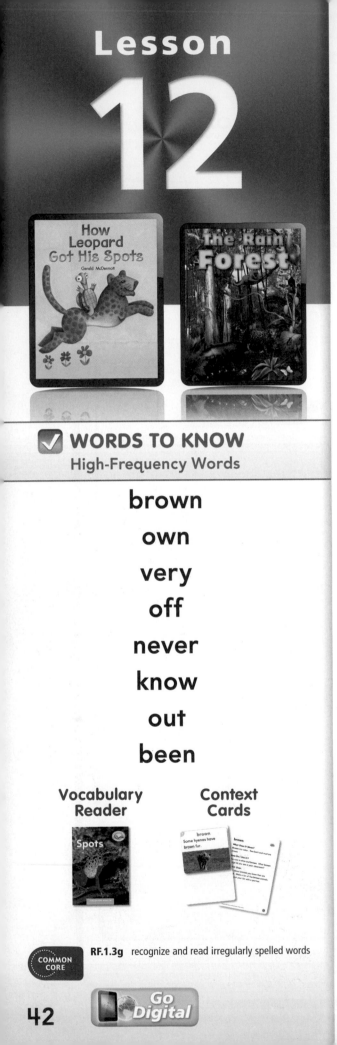

How Leopard Got His Spots
Gerald McDermott

The Rain Forest

✓ WORDS TO KNOW
High-Frequency Words

brown

own

very

off

never

know

out

been

Vocabulary Reader

Context Cards

Spots

RF.1.3g recognize and read irregularly spelled words

COMMON CORE

Go Digital

Words to Know

Read Together

▶ Read each Context Card.

▶ Describe a picture, using the blue word.

1

brown

Some hyenas have brown fur.

2

own

Zebras know their own mother by her stripes.

3 very

The snake in that tree is **very** long.

4 off

The bird flew **off** the rock and into the air.

5 never

Rhinos eat plants. They **never** eat meat.

6 know

Leopards **know** how to climb trees.

7 out

I called **out** to Mom, "Look at that turtle!"

8 been

The giraffes have **been** moving fast.

Read and Comprehend

☑ **TARGET SKILL**

Sequence of Events Most story events are told in time order. This order is called the **sequence of events.** Good readers think about what happens **first, next,** and **last** so that a story makes sense. You can describe the sequence of events in a flow chart like this.

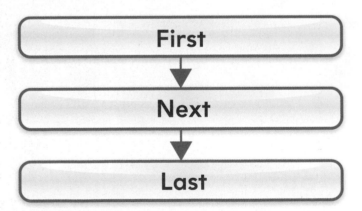

First

↓

Next

↓

Last

☑ **TARGET STRATEGY**

Question Ask yourself questions as you read. Look for text evidence to answer.

COMMON CORE **RL.1.1** ask and answer questions about key details; **RL.1.3** describe characters, settings, and major events

Jungle Animals

Many animals live in the jungle. Monkeys swing on vines. Frogs and snakes hide in the bushes. Birds fly through the trees. Which jungle animal is your favorite? You will read about jungle animals in **How Leopard Got His Spots.**

ANCHOR TEXT

How
Leopard
Got His Spots
Gerald McDermott

Sequence of Events
Tell the order in which things happen.

A **folktale** is an old story people have told for many years. As you read, look for:

▶ a lesson about life
▶ the words **once upon a time**

COMMON CORE **RL.1.2** retell stories and demonstrate understanding of the message or lesson; **RL.1.3** describe characters, settings, and major events; **RL.1.10** read prose and poetry

46 Go Digital

Meet the Author and Illustrator

Gerald McDermott

When Gerald McDermott was just four years old, he started taking art lessons at a museum. Saturdays were spent at the museum drawing, painting, and looking at the artwork. Mr. McDermott's book **Arrow to the Sun** won the Caldecott Medal for best illustrations.

How Leopard Got His Spots

written and illustrated by Gerald McDermott

ESSENTIAL QUESTION

How are jungle animals different from animals on a farm?

Do you know how
Leopard got his spots?

Once upon a time, Fred
Turtle was playing catch with
Hal Hyena. Hal tricked Fred.
Then he ran away.

Fred felt very sad.
He called out for help.
"Help! I am stuck in
the plants," he yelled.

Len Leopard ran to help.

Chop! Chop! Chop!
Len cut the plants off and
let Fred out.

Fred and Len danced in the sun.
"This is such fun!" they said.

"I have never been this glad,"
said Fred. "I like to paint if I
am glad!"

Fred mixed paints from many
flowers. Then he painted
black stripes on Zel Zebra.

Fred painted Jill Giraffe next.
"Look at me!" said Jill.
"I have big brown spots now."

"I like spots very much.
Can I have spots, too?"
asked Len.

Fred got set to paint Len.

"I like spots very much.
Can I have spots, too?"
asked Len.

Fred got set to paint Len.

Now Len had spots
of his very own.

Zel, Jill, and Len had such
fun looking at their spots
and stripes.
Hal said, "Paint me, too!"

But Fred had a trick for Hal.
He splashed Hal with brown
paint. Hal yelled and ran off.

Now Fred and Len
are best friends.

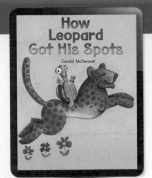

Dig Deeper

How to Analyze the Text

Use these pages to learn more about Sequence of Events and Story Lesson. Then read **How Leopard Got His Spots** again.

Sequence of Events

In **How Leopard Got His Spots,** Fred Turtle helps Len Leopard get his spots. Think about the important events in the story. What happens **first**, **next**, and **last?** This order is called the **sequence of events**. Use a flow chart like this to describe the order of events in the story.

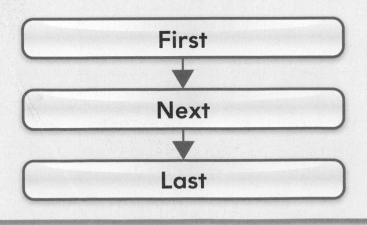

```
┌──────────────┐
│    First     │
└──────────────┘
        │
        ▼
┌──────────────┐
│    Next      │
└──────────────┘
        │
        ▼
┌──────────────┐
│    Last      │
└──────────────┘
```

RL.1.2 retell stories and demonstrate understanding of the message or lesson; **RL.1.3** describe characters, settings, and major events

Story Lesson

How Leopard Got His Spots is a folktale. People told this story for many years before it was written down. Folktales often teach a lesson. What lesson do you learn from Hal Hyena?

Folktales can also tell why something is the way it is. Think about Len Leopard's spots. What does this folktale try to explain?

Your Turn

RETURN TO THE ESSENTIAL QUESTION

 **Turn and Talk**

How are jungle animals different from animals on a farm? Use the words and pictures in the story to describe the jungle animals. Then draw a jungle animal and a farm animal. Take turns telling how the animals are different.

Classroom Conversation

Now talk about these questions with your class.

1. How does Len Leopard help Fred Turtle?

2. Why does Fred splash paint on Hal?

3. What do you think will happen the next time Hal Hyena sees the other animals?

Response Write the story the way Hal Hyena would tell it. Write sentences to tell what happens in the beginning, middle, and end of the story.

First

Next

Last

Writing Tip

Add words like **first**, **next**, and **last** to tell the events in order.

COMMON CORE **RL.1.1** ask and answer questions about key details; **RL.1.2** retell stories and demonstrate understanding of the message or lesson; **RL.1.7** use illustrations and details to describe characters, setting, or events; **W.1.3** write narratives; **SL.1.1a** follow rules for discussions

Read Together

The Rain Forest

COMMON CORE **RI.1.5** know and use text features to locate facts or information; **RI.1.10** read informational texts

Go Digital

The Rain Forest

A rain forest is a very wet and warm place. Rain forests have layers. Each layer has its own animals that live in it.

Canopy Layer The tops of trees poking out above the forest form this layer. The tree leaves and branches keep most sunlight off the layers below. Eagles, sloths, and monkeys live here.

Understory Layer This layer is above the ground. It is shady. Young trees and bushes grow here. Frogs, birds, and snakes live here.

sloth

eagle

monkey

toucan

jaguar

tapir

Forest Floor Not much sunlight reaches this layer. Tapirs, jaguars, and beetles live on the brown forest floor. Ants and giant anteaters also live there. Anteaters have been known to eat thirty thousand insects in a single day!

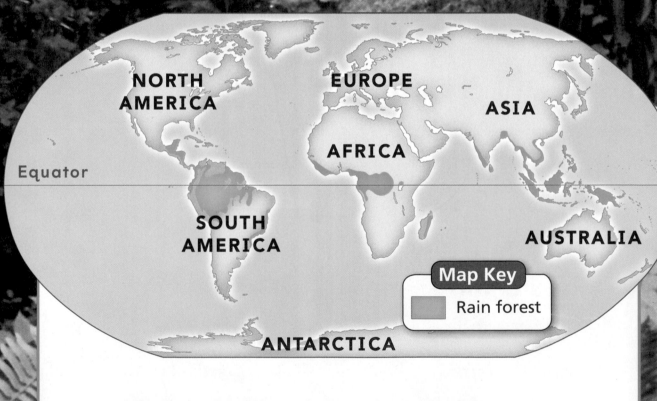

Do you know where the world's rain forests are? This map shows you.

Compare Texts

Read Together

TEXT TO TEXT

Compare Settings Look at both selections. Tell how the settings are alike and different. Make a chart.

Alike	Different

TEXT TO SELF

Write a Story What does **once upon a time** mean? Write a story about an animal you might see near your home. Begin your story with **once upon a time**.

TEXT TO WORLD

Make a Map Pretend that you are going to visit a rain forest. Draw a map showing where you will go. Explain any symbols or words you use on your map.

COMMON CORE **RL.1.3** describe characters, settings, and major events; **RI.1.3** describe the connection between individuals, events, ideas, or information in a text; **RI.1.5** know and use text features to locate facts or information; **W.1.3** write narratives; **L.1.6** use words and phrases acquired through conversations, reading and being read to, and responding to texts

Grammar

Commands A sentence that tells someone to do something is a **command**. A command can end with a period. A command can end with an exclamation point when it is said with strong feeling.

Commands
Pick up that pencil.
Draw stripes on the zebra.
Help the turtle right now!
Save the rain forest!

72

Read the sentences. Decide which ones are commands. Write each command on another sheet of paper. Then read the commands to a partner to check them.

1. Paint more spots on the giraffe.

2. Does the leopard like his spots?

3. Stand still while you paint.

4. Those paints are new.

5. Stay away from that wet paint!

Grammar in Writing

When you proofread your writing, be sure you have written commands correctly.

COMMON CORE W.1.2 write informative/explanatory texts; **L.1.1j** produce and expand simple and compound declarative, interrogative, imperative, and exclamatory sentences

Informative Writing

✓ **Sentence Fluency** In good **instructions**, the sentences tell the steps in order. Order words help make the steps easy to follow.

Akil drafted his instructions in a letter to his friend Pam. Later, he added the order word **Last**.

Read Together

my WriteSmart

Go Digital

Revised Draft

Last,
4. ~~C~~olor brown spots.
  ^

Writing Traits Checklist

✓ **Sentence Fluency** Do my instructions have order words?

✓ Did I tell the steps in order?

✓ Did I include a greeting and a closing in my letter?

Revise your writing using the Checklist. You can follow the instructions in Akil's final copy to make a puppet!

Final Copy

Dear Pam,

I made a leopard puppet. Here is how you can make one, too.

1. First, get a small paper bag.
2. Next, fold the sides of the flap.
3. Then, glue on ears, eyes, a nose, and whiskers.
4. Last, color brown spots.

I hope you have fun making your puppet.

Your friend,
Akil

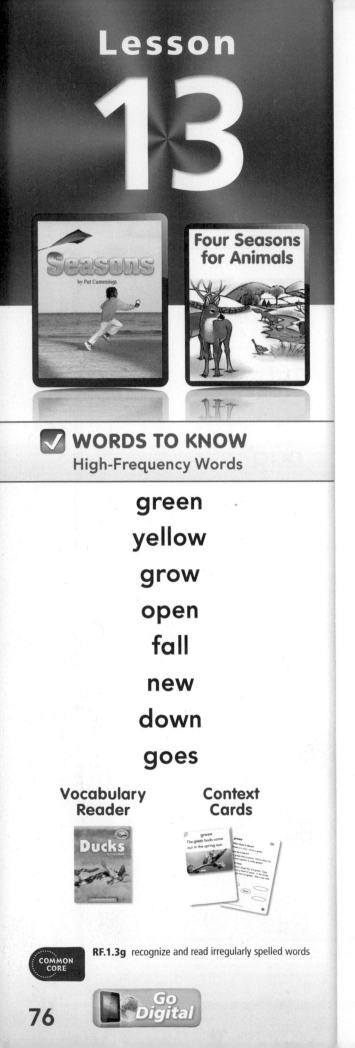

Seasons
by Pat Cummings

Four Seasons
for Animals

☑ **WORDS TO KNOW**
High-Frequency Words

green

yellow

grow

open

fall

new

down

goes

Vocabulary Reader

Context Cards

Ducks

COMMON CORE **RF.1.3g** recognize and read irregularly spelled words

Go Digital

Words to Know

Read Together

▶ Read each **Context Card**.

▶ Choose two blue words. Use them in sentences.

1 **green**

The green buds come out in the spring sun.

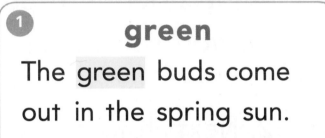

2 **yellow**

He put on yellow boots on a rainy day.

3 grow

Many flowers grow in the summer.

4 open

The windows can be open on a hot day.

5 fall

The leaves change color in fall.

6 new

She has a brand new backpack for school.

7 down

Snow comes down on a cold day.

8 goes

She goes to the park to skate with her mom.

Seasons
by Pat Cummings

Read and Comprehend

Read Together

Go Digital

☑ **TARGET SKILL**

Cause and Effect Sometimes one event can **cause** another event to happen. The **cause** happens first. It makes something else happen. The **effect** is what happens next. As you read, think about what happens and why. You can use a chart like this to show how events are connected.

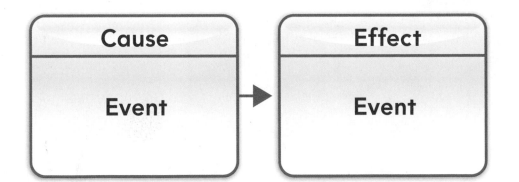

Cause	Effect
Event	Event

☑ **TARGET STRATEGY**

Visualize To understand a selection, picture events in your mind as you read.

COMMON CORE

RI.1.3 describe the connection between individuals, events, ideas, or information in a text

There are four seasons. In winter it is cold. It snows in some places. Then it gets warmer, and the snow melts. It becomes spring. In spring, plants begin to grow. Summer comes next. It gets hot. Then in fall, the leaves turn colors. It is cool. After fall, winter comes again!

You will read about how the weather changes each year in **Seasons**.

ANCHOR TEXT

Seasons
by Pat Cummings

✓ **TARGET SKILL**

Cause and Effect
Tell what happens and why.

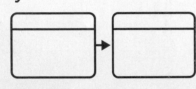

✓ **GENRE**

Informational text
gives facts about a topic. As you read, look for:
▶ information and facts in the words
▶ photos that show the real world

COMMON CORE **RI.1.3** describe the connection between individuals, events, ideas, or information in a text; **RI.1.4** ask and answer questions to determine or clarify the meaning of words and phrases; **RI.1.10** read informational texts

Meet the Author

Pat Cummings

Pat Cummings loves getting letters from kids who have read her books. Sometimes they send her other things too, such as T-shirts, mugs, drawings, and even science projects. **Clean Your Room, Harvey Moon!** is just one of her many books.

Seasons

written by Pat Cummings

Spring

In the spring,
fresh winds blow.
We plant new seeds,
and green buds grow.

Eggs hatch open.
Little chicks sing.
The sun is out.
It must be spring!

The grass gets wet.

Splish! Splash! Splish!

When we step,

we hear it squish.

Summer

Then summer is here
and it gets hot.
We are not in school.
We play a lot.

Bugs buzz and hum.
The plants grow tall.
Next to them,
I look small.

Summer goes fast,
and when it ends,
we will go back to school
with all our friends.

Fall

In fall the leaves
are red, yellow, and brown.
In a gust of wind,
they will fall down.

The leaves crunch
as we jump and hop.
It is such fun,
we cannot stop!

Animals get nuts
and pack them away.
They will have lots to eat
on a cold day.

Winter

When it is winter,
cold winds blow.
It is fun to sled
on the soft snow.

When it is cold,
some animals rest.
This animal has
a nap in a nest.

A hat on a shelf
gives us a plan.
We will put the hat
on a big snowman!

Winter

Spring

Summer

Winter, Spring,
Summer, Fall.
Which is best?
We like them all!

Fall

Dig Deeper

How to Analyze the Text

Use these pages to learn about Cause and Effect and Sound Words. Then read **Seasons** again.

Cause and Effect

In **Seasons**, many events cause other events to happen. The **cause** happens first. It is the reason why something else happens. The **effect** is what happens next. In **Seasons**, you read that it is cold in winter. What does the cold cause some animals to do? Use a chart to show what happens and why.

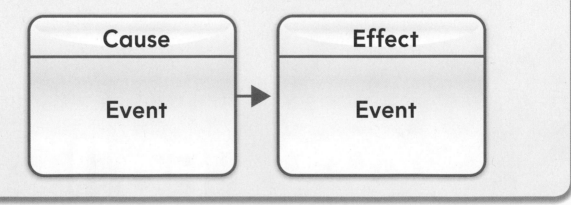

Cause	Effect
Event	Event

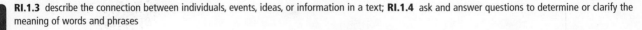

Sound Words

An author can use words that sound like real noises. In the part about spring, the author uses the words **Splish! Splash! Splish!** These words describe the sounds of rain and wet grass.

Find other words that tell about sounds in **Seasons.** Ask yourself what the words mean and what they describe. Use the other words and sentences to help you. Do sound words help you know what real things are like?

Your Turn

RETURN TO THE ESSENTIAL QUESTION

 **Turn and Talk**

What changes do the different seasons cause?
Talk with a partner about why changes happen in each season. Then look for text evidence to explain your answer. Take turns.

Classroom Conversation

Talk about these questions with your class.

1 What do animals do in different seasons?

2 How do plants change from spring to summer to fall?

3 Tell what the seasons are like where you live.

WRITE ABOUT READING

Response Write about your favorite season. First, tell what your topic is. Then give reasons why you like the season. Use text evidence from **Seasons** for ideas. Write an ending sentence.

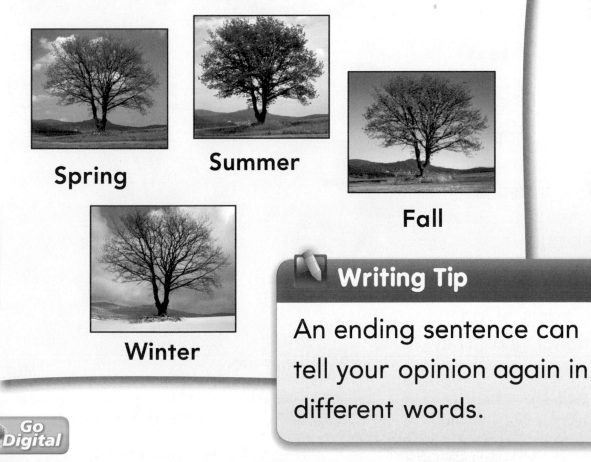

Spring

Summer

Fall

Winter

Writing Tip

An ending sentence can tell your opinion again in different words.

COMMON CORE **RI.1.1** ask and answer questions about key details; **RI.1.3** describe the connection between individuals, events, ideas, or information in a text; **W.1.1** write opinion pieces; **SL.1.1a** follow rules for discussions

INFORMATIONAL TEXT

Read Together

Four Seasons for Animals

GENRE

Informational text gives facts about a topic. Look for facts about what happens to plants and animals during the seasons.

TEXT FOCUS

Headings are titles for different parts of an informational text. They tell you what each section will be about. What do the headings in this selection tell you?

RI.1.5 know and use text features to locate facts or information; **RI.1.10** read informational texts

Four Seasons for Animals

written and illustrated
by Ashley Wolff

Spring

It is spring. Young animals run and play. Bird nests are full of eggs. Soon the eggs will hatch.

Spring brings rain. Grass turns green and grows tall. Buds grow on trees and plants. Spring also brings rain puddles! Flower buds get wet. Rain helps the new plants grow.

Summer

It is summer. Buds open and flowers bloom in the bright sun. Insects buzz here and there. Now there are chicks in the bird nest! Their mother will teach them how to fly.

It can get very hot in the summer.
Many animals live near the pond.
Ducks swim in the pond. Fox pups
cool off in the shade.

Fall

It is fall. Leaves fall down. Animals get ready for winter. Some animals eat as much as they can. They need to store fat because food is scarce in the winter.

Squirrels and chipmunks gather nuts
so they will have enough food for
the winter.

Winter

It is winter. Winter can be very cold
and wet. Bears hibernate in the winter.
That means they sleep.

Many other animals hibernate in the winter. They curl up in dens to keep safe from the cold and wet.

Like all the seasons, the winter will
pass. The animals know that spring
will come once again.

Compare Texts

Read Together

TEXT TO TEXT

Make a Chart How are the selections alike and different? Make a chart to show evidence.

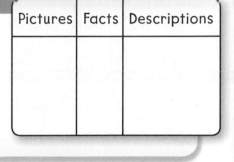

Pictures	Facts	Descriptions

TEXT TO SELF

Describe a Season Describe your favorite season. Tell why you like it. Use details to make your ideas and feelings clear.

TEXT TO WORLD

Tell About Seasons Find your state on a globe. Then locate a country. Tell how you think the seasons in both places might be the same or different.

COMMON CORE RI.1.3 describe the connection between individuals, events, ideas, or information in a text; RI.1.9 identify similarities in and differences between texts on the same topic; SL.1.4 describe people, places, things, and events with details/express ideas and feelings clearly

Grammar

Subjects and Verbs In a sentence, the subject and the verb have to agree. Both must tell about the same number of people or things. Add **s** to most **verbs** when they tell about a **noun** that names one.

One	More Than One
One **boy pulls** his sled.	Two **girls pull** their dog.
Brett slides down the hill.	**Children slide** across the pond.

116

Choose the correct verb to finish each sentence. Take turns reading a sentence aloud with a partner. Then talk about how you chose the correct verb.

1. Raindrops _____?_____ each spring.

fall   falls

2. Flowers _____?_____ in the garden.

grow   grows

3. One bug _____?_____ all night.

hum   hums

4. Now the sun _____?_____ brightly.

shine   shines

5. The children _____?_____ in the pool.

swim   swims

Grammar in Writing

When you proofread your writing, be sure you have written the correct verb to go with each noun.

COMMON CORE W.1.2 write informative/explanatory texts; **W.1.5** focus on a topic, respond to questions/suggestions from peers, and add details to strengthen writing; **L.1.1c** use singular and plural nouns with matching verbs in sentences

Informative Writing

☑ **Ideas**   When you write **sentences** that tell facts, be sure all your sentences are about one main idea.

Kyle wrote about winter. Then he took out a sentence that didn't belong.

Revised Draft

Winter is the coldest season.

Sometimes it snows here.

~~I have a dog.~~

 Writing Traits Checklist

Ideas   Are all my sentences about one main idea? Do the details tell facts?

☑ Did I write the correct verb to go with each noun?

  Did I write a good ending sentence?

118

Look for the main idea sentence in Kyle's final copy. Then revise your writing. Use the Checklist.

Final Copy

A Chilly Season

Winter is the coldest season.
Sometimes it snows here.
We go sledding.
The lake freezes.
People skate on it.
Winter is cold, but you can
still go out and play.

The Big Race
written by Pam Muñoz Ryan
illustrated by Viviana Garofoli

Rules and Laws

POLICE

☑ **WORDS TO KNOW**
High-Frequency Words

two

into

three

starts

over

four

five

watch

Vocabulary Reader

Desert Animals

Context Cards

two
Two desert lizards are sitting on the rock.

RF.1.3g recognize and read irregularly spelled words

COMMON CORE

Go Digital

Words to Know

Read Together

▶ Read each **Context Card**.

▶ Use a blue word to tell about something you did.

1 **two**

Two desert lizards are sitting on the rock.

2 **into**

The bird flew into the big cactus.

3 three

There are three birds resting in the sun.

4 starts

The desert starts to cool down at sunset.

5 over

A hawk flew over the tall rocks.

6 four

All four legs of this fox are strong.

7 five

This desert flower has five red spots.

8 watch

The rabbits watch and listen for danger.

Read and Comprehend

The Big Race

written by Pam Muñoz Ryan
illustrated by Viviana Garofoli

Read Together

Go Digital

Conclusions Sometimes authors do not tell all the details in a story. Readers must use clues in the words and pictures and think about what they already know. This will help them make a smart guess about what the author does not tell. This smart guess is a **conclusion**. Use a chart to list the clues and your conclusions.

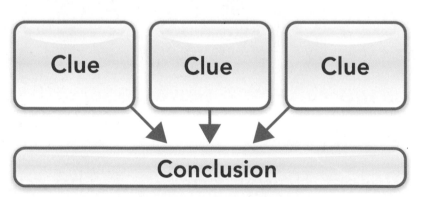

Infer/Predict Use text evidence to help you think of what might happen next.

RL.1.3 describe characters, settings, and major events; **RL.1.7** use illustrations and details to describe characters, setting, or events

COMMON CORE

122

Citizenship

Cross at the cross walk. This rule keeps you safe. **Wash your hands.** This rule keeps you healthy. Following rules makes you a good classmate. It makes you a good neighbor, too. What rules do you follow at school? What rules do you follow at home? What rules do you follow when you play?

When you read **The Big Race,** think about the rules and the different ways the animals race.

ANCHOR TEXT

The
Big Race
written by Pam Muñoz Ryan
illustrated by Viviana Garofoli

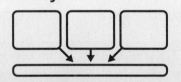

☑ **TARGET SKILL**

Conclusions Use clues and what you know to figure out more about a story.

☑ **GENRE**

A **fantasy** could not happen in real life. As you read, look for:
▶ animals who talk and act like people
▶ events that could not really happen

 COMMON CORE **RL.1.3** describe characters, settings, and major events; **RL.1.7** use illustrations and details to describe characters, setting, or events; **RL.1.10** read prose and poetry

  Go Digital

Meet the Author

Pam Muñoz Ryan

California summers can be very hot. When Pam Muñoz Ryan was growing up, she was often at the library on summer days. That's because the library was one of the few places nearby with air conditioning!

Meet the Illustrator

Viviana Garofoli

Viviana Garofoli and her family make their home in the country of Argentina. **Sophie's Trophy** and **My Big Rig** are two of the books she has illustrated.

The Big Race

written by Pam Muñoz Ryan

illustrated by Viviana Garofoli

Win the Big Race
Win this Big Cake

Today is the big race.

"I like cake!" said Red Lizard.
"I will run in that race."

Red Lizard gets to the race.
Four animals will run with him.

Cottontail is not late.

She will run in lane one.

Rat naps in the shade.

She will run in lane two.

Snake takes his spot in lane three.

Roadrunner stands in lane four.

He waves to his pals.

Red Lizard is in lane five.

The animals bend and hop.

The flag is down, and the race starts!
Many animals watch and clap.

Cottontail does not get far.

Rat falls into the hay.

Snake stops and chases bugs.

Roadrunner trips over a rake.

Who will win?

It's Red Lizard who wins!

"Watch me eat this cake," he yells.
Red Lizard looks at his big cake.

Red Lizard looks at his pals.

His pals like cake, too.
What will Red Lizard do now?

Red Lizard gets five plates.

He gets cake for his pals, too.

Hip, Hip, Hooray for Red Lizard!

COMPREHENSION

Dig Deeper

Read Together

How to Analyze the Text

Use these pages to learn about
Conclusions and Cause and Effect.
Then read **The Big Race** again.

Conclusions

You can use clues in **The Big Race** to
think about things the author does not say.
The author does not tell you why Cottontail
does not win. What do the pictures and
words show that help you make a smart
guess about why? What do you know
about races that helps you understand?
Use a chart to list clues and conclusions.

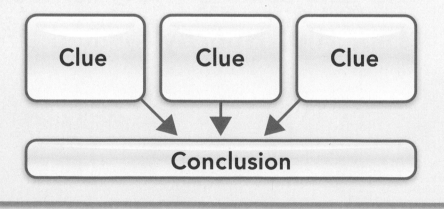

Clue   Clue   Clue

Conclusion

RL.1.3 describe characters, settings, and major events; **RL.1.7** use illustrations and details to describe characters, setting, or events

COMMON CORE

Cause and Effect

Sometimes one event in a story causes another event to happen. As you read, ask yourself what happens and why.

In **The Big Race**, why doesn't Snake win? He does not win because he stops to chase bugs. Snake stopping is the **cause**. What happens after that? Snake loses the race. That is the **effect**.

Your Turn

 my WriteSmart

RETURN TO THE ESSENTIAL QUESTION

 Turn and Talk

Why is it important to have rules? Describe what happens to the animals in the story when they do not follow the rules. Use text evidence to help you answer. Speak in complete sentences.

💬 **Classroom Conversation**

Talk about these questions with your class.

1 Why does Red Lizard win the race?

2 How does Red Lizard feel when he wins?

3 Red Lizard shares the cake. Is this the right thing to do? Why or why not?

Response Choose a favorite character from **The Big Race**. Write sentences to give reasons why you like him or her. Use details from the story to explain your opinion.

Writing Tip

Use **because** to tell why you think something is true.

COMMON CORE   **RL.1.1** ask and answer questions about key details; **RL.1.7** use illustrations and details to describe characters, setting, or events; **W.1.1** write opinion pieces; **SL.1.4** describe people, places, things, and events with details/express ideas and feelings clearly; **SL.1.6** produce complete sentences when appropriate to task and situation

Read Together

Rules and Laws

GENRE

Informational text gives facts on a topic. It can be from a textbook, article, or website. Look for facts about rules and laws as you read.

TEXT FOCUS

Labels are words that tell more about a picture or photo. They can name parts of or the whole picture. What information do the labels in this selection give?

COMMON CORE **RI.1.5** know and use text features to locate facts or information; **RI.1.10** read informational texts .

Rules and Laws

by J. C. Cunningham

Health Rule

Rules

Who needs rules? We all do! Some rules keep us safe and healthy. Some rules help us learn. There are even rules to help us have fun!

Safety Rule

Can you find the child following this rule? **Raise your hand to speak.** What other rules are the children following? What could happen if they did not follow the rules?

School Rule

Game Rule

Laws

Our government has rules, too. The rules are called laws. Laws keep us safe and healthy. Laws make sure we treat each other fairly.

EMPLOYEES MUST WASH HANDS

Can you find the person who obeyed this law?
Employees must wash hands.
What other laws do you think the pictures show?

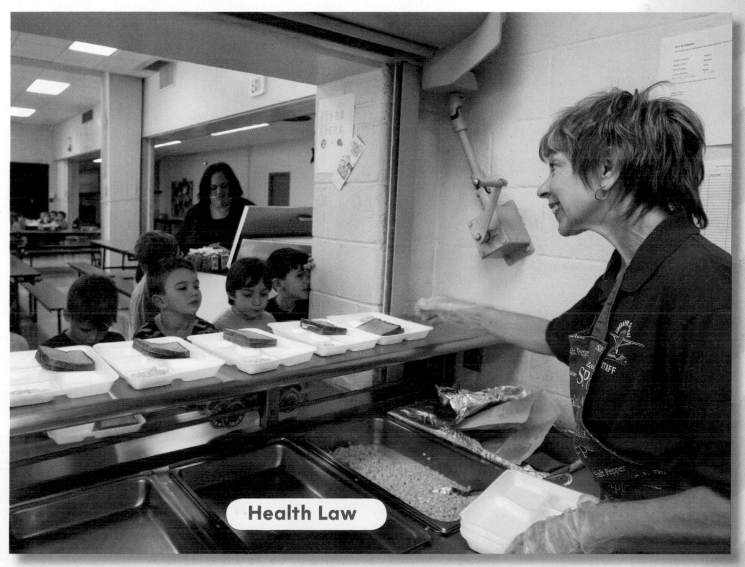

Health Law

Laws help us to be good neighbors and good citizens.

What laws do you think these people are following? How do the laws help?

Who needs
rules and laws?
We all do!

Compare Texts

Read Together

TEXT TO TEXT

Compare Stories Think about the selections. Which is real and which is make-believe? Tell how you know. Take turns sharing evidence with a partner.

TEXT TO SELF

Write a List Write a list of rules the runners should follow in **The Big Race**. Tell why the rules make sense.

TEXT TO WORLD

Map a Race Course Pretend you will run a race through your neighborhood. Where does the race begin? Where is the finish line? Draw a map.

COMMON CORE **RL.1.5** explain major differences between story books and informational books; **W.1.2** write informative/explanatory texts; **SL.1.1a** follow rules for discussions; **SL.1.1b** build on others' talk in conversations by responding to others' comments

Grammar

Verbs and Time Some **verbs** tell what is happening now. Some verbs tell what happened in the past. Add **ed** to most verbs to tell about the past.

Now	In the Past
The **animals watch** the race now.	The **animals watched** the race yesterday.
They cheer for their friends.	**They cheered** for their friends.

156

**Try This!**

Work with a partner. One partner reads aloud a sentence. The other partner finds the verb. Together, write the verb to tell about the past. Take turns.

1. The runners look at the flag.

2. They start the race.

3. Some racers jump high.

4. They finish the race quickly.

5. The winners pick prizes.

Grammar in Writing

When you proofread your writing, be sure each verb tells clearly if something is happening now or in the past.

W.1.2 write informative/explanatory texts; **W.1.5** focus on a topic, respond to questions/suggestions from peers, and add details to strengthen writing; **W.1.7** participate in shared research and writing projects; **W.1.8** recall information from experiences or gather information from sources to answer a question

Reading-Writing Workshop: Prewrite

Informative Writing

✓ **Ideas**   A good **report** needs facts! Before you write, find facts to answer the question you wrote about your topic. Lena found information about lizards. She took notes to remind her of the facts.

Exploring a Topic

Prewriting Checklist

✓ Did I write a good question about my topic?

✓ Will my notes help me remember the facts?

✓ Did I use good sources for information?

158

Look for facts in Lena's notes. Then record your own notes. Use the Checklist.

Planning Chart

My Question
What do real lizards do?

Fact 1
change color

Fact 2
run fast on back legs

Fact 3
puff up to look big

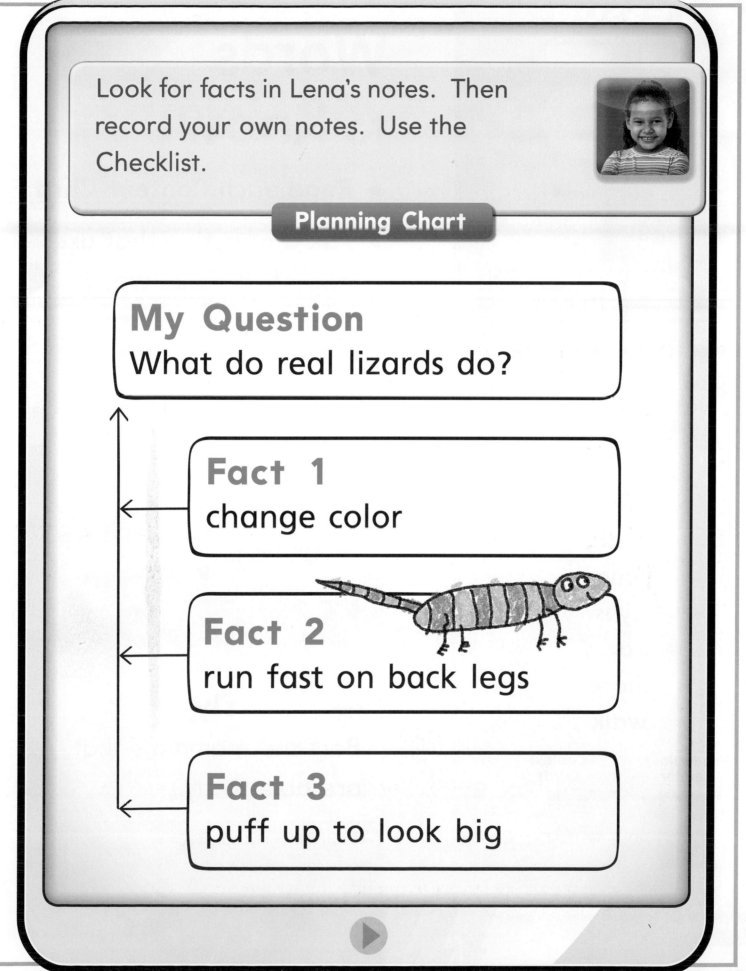

Animal
Groups
by James Bruchac

Animal
Picnic

✅ **WORDS TO KNOW**
High-Frequency Words

bird

fly

both

long

eyes

or

those

walk

**Vocabulary
Reader**

**Context
Cards**

COMMON
CORE

RF.1.3g recognize and read irregularly spelled words

Go
Digital

Words to Know

Read Together

▶ Read each **Context** Card.

▶ Ask a question that uses one of the blue words.

1 **bird**

An eagle is a bird with big, strong wings.

2 **fly**

Bats are mammals that are able to fly.

3 both

The lizard has **both** stripes and spots.

4 long

This kangaroo has a **long** tail.

5 eyes

This dog has blue **eyes**.

6 or

Ducks can either swim **or** fly.

7 those

Those fish are not the same colors.

8 walk

The elephants **walk** together in a group.

Animal Groups
by James Bruchac

Read and Comprehend

Read Together

Go Digital

☑ **TARGET SKILL**

Compare and Contrast When you **compare**, tell how things are alike. When you **contrast**, tell how things are different. Think about how things are alike and different to understand a selection better. You can use a diagram to **compare** and **contrast** two things.

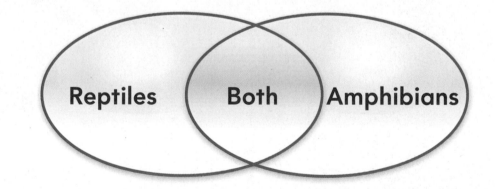

Reptiles — Both — Amphibians

☑ **TARGET STRATEGY**

Monitor/Clarify If a word or a part does not make sense, you can ask questions, reread, or use the pictures for help.

 COMMON CORE **RI.1.3** describe the connection between individuals, events, ideas, or information in a text; **RI.1.4** ask and answer questions to determine or clarify the meaning of words and phrases

Animals

All birds have wings, but not all birds fly. Some animals have legs and some do not. Fish live in water all the time. Other animals live on land.

Animals are alike and different. What animals do you know about? You will read about how animals are alike and different in **Animal Groups.**

ANCHOR TEXT

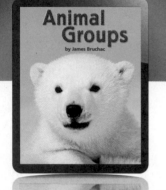

Animal Groups
by James Bruchac

Compare and Contrast
Tell how two things are alike and different.

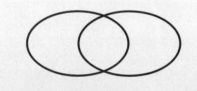

Informational text gives facts about a topic. As you read, look for:

► information and facts in the words
► photos that show the real world

COMMON CORE **RI.1.3** describe the connection between individuals, events, ideas, or information in a text; **RI.1.7** use illustrations and details to describe key ideas; **RI.1.10** read informational texts

Meet the Author

James Bruchac

James Bruchac has many interests. He is a writer, a storyteller, an animal tracker, and a wilderness guide. Together with his father, Joseph Bruchac, he wrote the books **How Chipmunk Got His Stripes** and **Turtle's Race with Beaver**.

Animal Groups

written by James Bruchac

ESSENTIAL QUESTION

What makes birds different from mammals?

Fish

Amphibian

Reptile

Let's take a look at five animal groups.

Bird

Mammal

How are animals in a group the same?

Fish

fin

eye

mouth

gill

fin

Fish must live in water. Fish have gills that help them breathe in water.

tail

Fish have fins and tails. Those help
them swim.

Fish can be many shapes and sizes.
Can you find a fish in this picture?

Reptiles

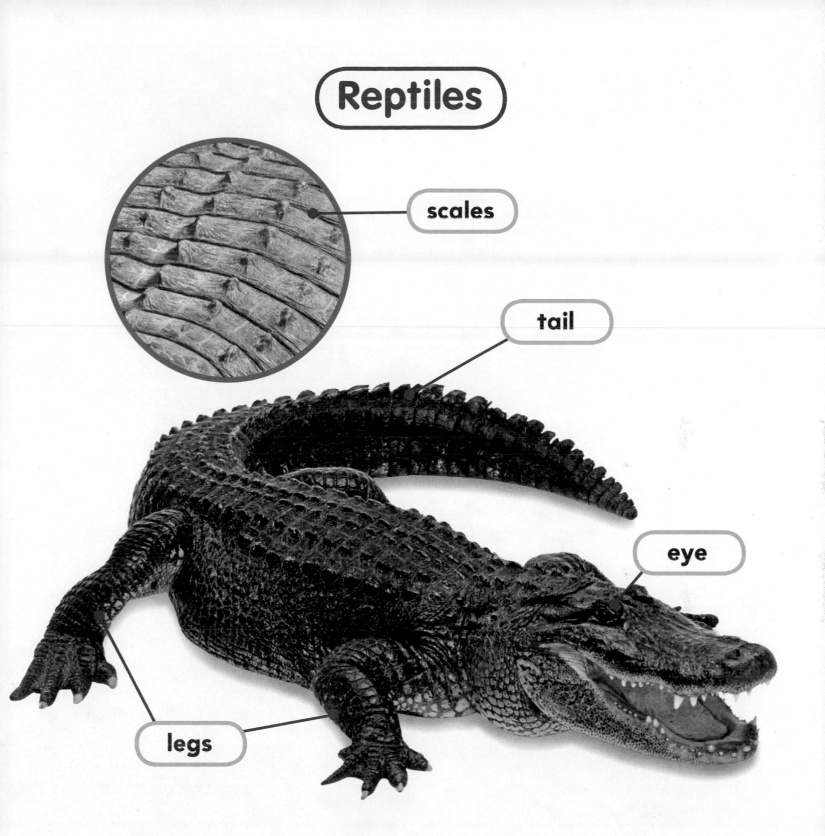

scales

tail

eye

legs

Reptiles can live on land. Some like to be in water. Reptiles have scales on their skin.

Many reptiles hatch from eggs.

Snakes cannot walk. They do not
have legs. This snake slides its long
body on the grass.

Amphibians

eye

wet skin

legs

Amphibians spend time both on land
and in water. They do not have scales.
Their skin is wet.

tadpoles

Amphibians hatch from eggs.
Tadpoles hatch and grow to be frogs.

Birds

eye

bill

wing

feathers

A bird has feathers and wings. This
bird's eyes are on the sides of its face!

Many birds can fly. Some can run
or swim fast.

Birds hatch from eggs. This hen made a nest for its eggs.

Mammals

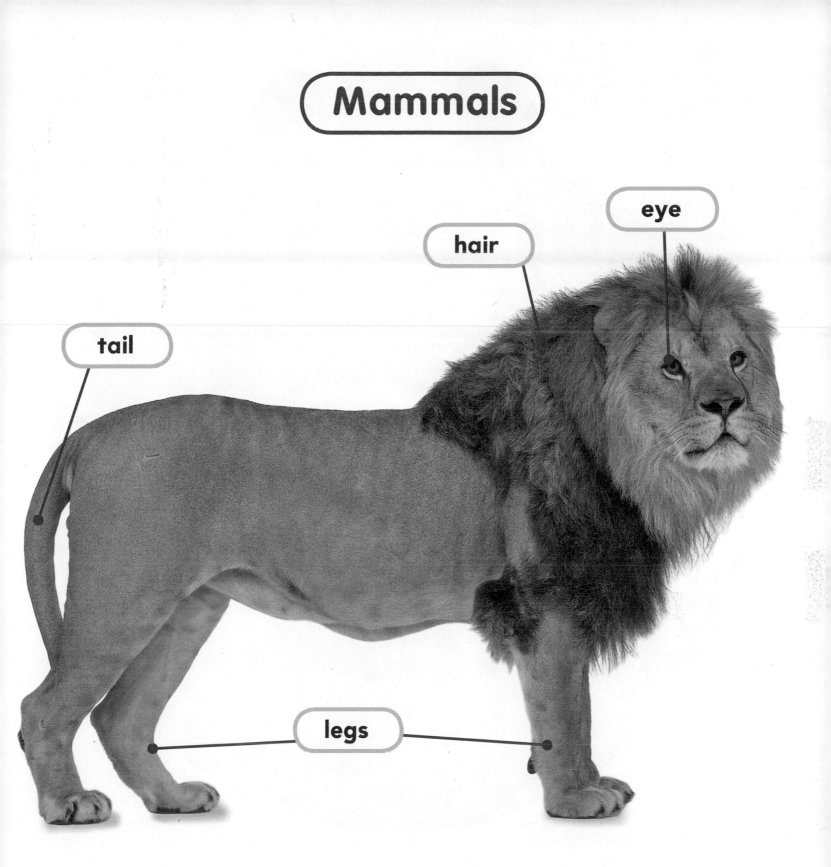

eye

hair

tail

legs

Mammals can be many shapes and sizes.
They have hair on their skin.

A mammal mom can
make milk for its baby.

Lots of mammals live on land,
but some live in water.

Did you know that you
are a mammal, too?

Dig Deeper

Read Together

How to Analyze the Text

Use these pages to learn about Compare and Contrast and Text and Graphic Features. Then read **Animal Groups** again.

Compare and Contrast

In **Animal Groups,** you learned what makes animals in a group the same and different. Think about reptiles and amphibians. **Compare** the groups to tell how they are alike. **Contrast** the groups to tell how they are different. Use a diagram to compare and contrast groups.

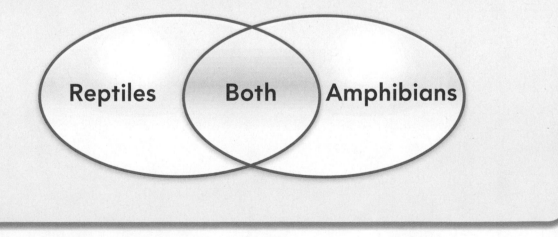

Reptiles   Both   Amphibians

COMMON CORE
RI.1.3 describe the connection between individuals, events, ideas, or information in a text; **RI.1.5** know and use text features to locate facts or information; **RI.1.7** use illustrations and details to describe key ideas

Go Digital

Text and Graphic Features

Authors use special features to point out information. **Headings** are often at the top of a page and tell what part you are reading. **Labels** are words that give more information about details in pictures.

The heading on page 168 is **Fish**. What is this part about? There are also labels that give information. What do you learn about a fish's body?

Your Turn

my WriteSmart

RETURN TO THE ESSENTIAL QUESTION

Turn and Talk

What makes birds different from mammals?
Choose an animal from each group. Use words and pictures from the selection to tell how the animals are alike and different. Ask questions if you do not understand your partner's ideas.

💬 Classroom Conversation

Talk about these questions with your class.

1 How are all mammals alike?

2 How are fish different from mammals?

3 What are the five animal groups? What new things did you learn?

WRITE ABOUT READING

Animal Groups
by James Bruchac

Response Use facts you learned from the selection to write a riddle about an animal. Write clues. Do not give its name. Read your riddle to a partner. Have your partner use the evidence in the clues to guess the answer.

I have gills and live in water.

Writing Tip

Use a question mark (?) at the end of a question.

Go Digital

COMMON CORE **RI.1.3** describe the connection between individuals, events, ideas, or information in a text; **RI.1.7** use illustrations and details to describe key ideas; **W.1.8** recall information from experiences or gather information from sources to answer a question; **SL.1.1c** ask questions to clear up confusion about topics and texts under discussion; **SL.1.3** ask and answer questions about what a speaker says

Read Together

Animal Picnic

✓ GENRE

A **play** is a story that people act out. Most of the words in a play are the words the characters say.

✓ TEXT FOCUS

Stage directions are extra words in a play that tell about the characters and setting. They also tell what actions characters do. What are the stage directions in this play? How do you know?

 COMMON CORE   **RL.1.10** read prose and poetry

 Go Digital

Animal Picnic

by Debbie O'Brien

Cast of Characters

Fox

Cow

Bird

 Hi, Cow and Bird. How was your trip?

 I had to walk to get here.

 I had to fly.

(pointing to Cow's basket)
What food did you bring for our picnic?

I brought grass. I use my flat teeth to grind it.

I brought meat. I use my long, sharp teeth to eat it.

We both have teeth, but we eat different things!

(pointing to Bird's basket)
What did you bring, Bird?

 I did not bring grass or meat.
I brought seeds. Birds don't
have any teeth!

 How will you eat those seeds
without teeth?

 Watch this!
(Bird eats some seeds.)
Yum, yum, yum!

Compare Texts

Read Together

TEXT TO TEXT

Compare Information Think about both selections. How are they alike and different? What information do you learn in each selection?

Alike	Different

TEXT TO SELF

Talk About Animals Which animal group is your favorite? Talk about it with a partner. Use complete sentences.

TEXT TO WORLD

Write a Question Write a question you have about an animal in the selections. Use this book or other books to find the answer.

COMMON CORE **RI.1.1** ask and answer questions about key details; **RI.1.9** identify similarities in and differences between texts on the same topic; **W.1.8** recall information from experiences or gather information from sources to answer a question; **SL.1.6** produce complete sentences when appropriate to task and situation

Grammar

The Verb be The verbs **is** and **are** tell what is happening now. Use **is** with a noun that names one.

One	More Than One
 This **chick** is small.	Two **chicks** are small.

The verbs **was** and **were** tell what happened in the past. Use **was** with a noun that names one.

One	More Than One
 One **egg** was here.	Two **eggs** were here.

Read each sentence aloud two times, saying a different verb each time. Ask your partner to repeat the sentence with the correct verb. Then switch roles.

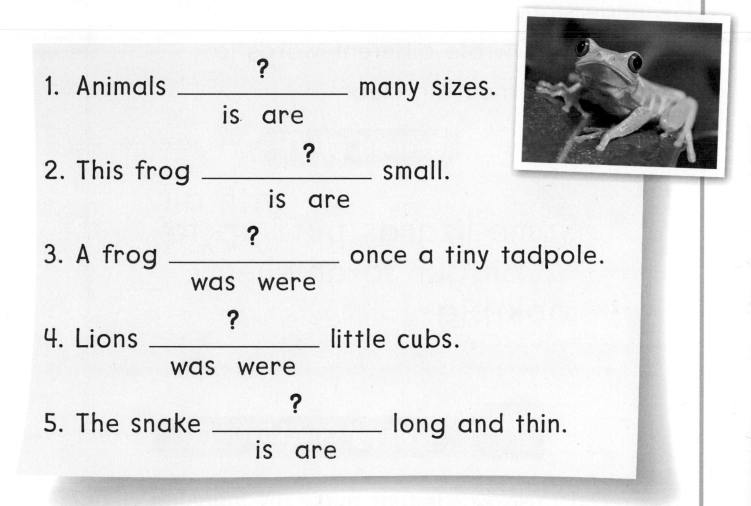

1. Animals _____ **?** many sizes.
   is are

2. This frog _____ **?** small.
   is are

3. A frog _____ **?** once a tiny tadpole.
   was were

4. Lions _____ **?** little cubs.
   was were

5. The snake _____ **?** long and thin.
   is are

🖊 Grammar in Writing

When you proofread your writing, be sure you have used the verbs **is**, **are**, **was**, and **were** correctly.

COMMON CORE W.1.2 write informative/explanatory texts; **W.1.5** focus on a topic, respond to questions/suggestions from peers, and add details to strengthen writing; **L.1.2b** use end punctuation for sentences; **L.1.2d** use conventional spelling for words with common spelling patterns and for frequently occurring irregular words

Reading-Writing Workshop: Revise

Informative Writing

✓ **Word Choice**   In a good **report**, the right words make the facts easy to understand. Lena drafted her report. Later, she wrote different words to make her meaning clear.

Read Together

my WriteSmart

Go Digital

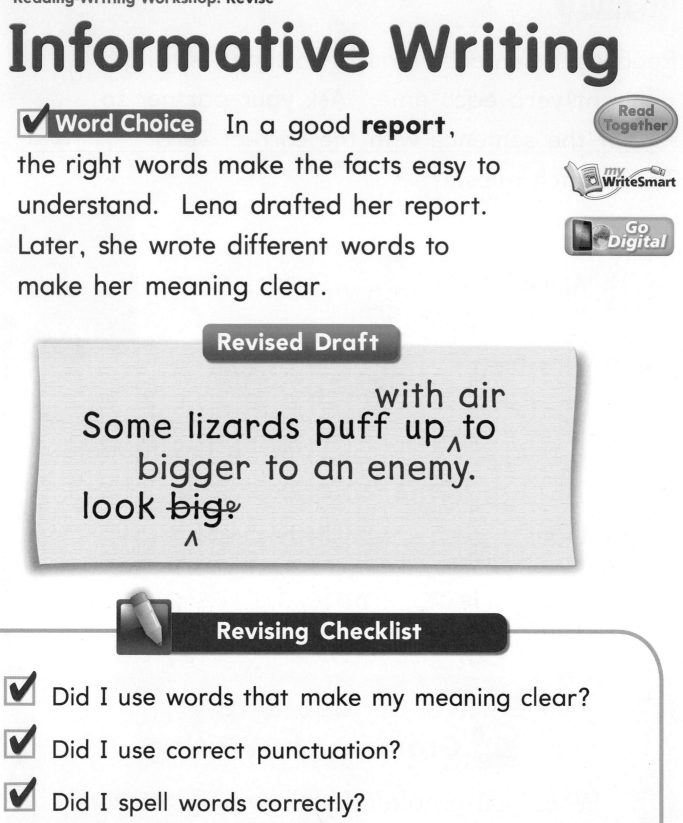

Revised Draft

Some lizards puff up to bigger to an enemy.
                      with air ∧
look big. ∧

Revising Checklist

✓ Did I use words that make my meaning clear?

✓ Did I use correct punctuation?

✓ Did I spell words correctly?

✓ Did I write a good ending sentence?

194

Final Copy

An Interesting Reptile

Lizards do some funny things. Some can change color quickly. Others run fast using only their back legs. Some lizards puff up with air to look bigger to an enemy. Lizards are very interesting reptiles.

Read Together

Read each article. As you read, stop and answer each question. Use text evidence.

Frogs and Toads

Frogs and toads are alike in some ways. They both lay eggs in water. They both live in water when they are small. They both eat lots of bugs.

 1 Where do frogs and toads live when they are small?

Frogs and toads are different in some ways, too. Frogs have smooth, wet skin. Frogs live in or near water. They have long back legs, too. This helps them hop and swim.

COMMON CORE

RI.1.1 ask and answer questions about key details; **RI.1.3** describe the connection between individuals, events, ideas, or information in a text; **RI.1.4** ask and answer questions to determine or clarify the meaning of words and phrases; **RI.1.8** identify the reasons an author gives to support points; **RI.1.10** read informational texts; **L.1.4a** use sentence-level context as a clue to the meaning of a word or phrase

Toads have dry, bumpy skin. Toads spend much of their time on land. They have small back legs. This helps them walk.

2 How are frogs different from toads?

 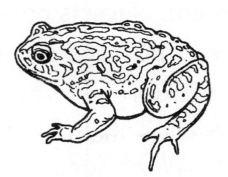

Roly-Poly Bugs

A pill bug is a very small animal. It is also called a roly-poly. It can roll into a little ball that looks like a pill. This helps keep it safe from danger.

> **❸** What does **danger** mean in this article? What words help you know?

Pill bugs hatch from eggs. They live in damp places. They live under leaves, rocks, or logs.

Some people think pill bugs are insects. They are not. Insects have six legs. Pill bugs have more. Pill bugs are in the same animal group as a crab!

> **❹** What does the author want you to learn? What details help you know?

Words to Know

Unit 3   High-Frequency Words

⑪ **At Home in the Ocean**

blue	where
far	water
live	cold
little	their

⑭ **The Big Race**

two	over
into	four
three	five
starts	watch

⑫ **How Leopard Got His Spots**

brown	never
own	know
very	out
off	been

⑮ **Animal Groups**

bird	eyes
fly	or
both	those
long	walk

⑬ **Seasons**

green	fall
yellow	new
grow	down
open	goes

Glossary

A

amphibians
An **amphibian** is an animal that lives in water and on land. Frogs are **amphibians**.

B

biggest
Something that is the **biggest** is bigger in size than anything else. The whale is the **biggest** animal in the ocean.

blow
To **blow** means to push air. The winds **blow** the cold air across the land.

body
The **body** of a person or animal is made up of the parts you can see and touch. We are learning about the parts of the **body**.

breathe

To **breathe** is to take in breaths of air. I **breathe** in the fresh air when I am outside.

C

cottontail

A **cottontail** is a kind of rabbit. That **cottontail** has a white fluffy tail.

D

danced

To **dance** means to move to music. We played music and **danced** for hours.

day

A **day** is the time from one morning to the next morning. Tuesday was a sunny **day**.

F

feathers

A **feather** is a part of a bird. The bird had soft **feathers**.

feet

A foot is a measurement that equals 12 inches. **Feet** means more than one foot. Some trees can grow as tall as 100 **feet**.

flowers

A **flower** is a part of a plant. We planted pretty **flowers** in the garden.

G

giraffe

A **giraffe** is a tall spotted animal with a long neck. The **giraffe** ate leaves from the top of the tree.

grow

When plants and animals **grow**, they get bigger and bigger. Kittens **grow** and become cats.

group

A **group** is a number of people or things together.
A **group** of us went swimming last Saturday.

H

hair

Hair is what grows on your head. My dad cuts my **hair**
when it gets too long.

hay

Hay is a kind of grass that
has been cut and dried.
My horse likes to eat **hay**.

home

A **home** is a place where people or animals live.
Jellyfish make their **home** underwater.

hooray

Hooray is something people shout when they are happy.
When I hit a home run, my parents yelled **hooray!**

hyena

A **hyena** is a wild animal that looks like a dog.
The **hyena** is found in Africa and Asia.

L

leaves

A **leaf** is a part of a plant. In the fall, the **leaves** turn pretty colors.

leopard

A **leopard** is a wild animal that looks like a cat with spots. The **leopard** paced in its cage.

lions

A **lion** is a large wild animal that looks like a big cat. We saw a movie about **lions** in Africa.

lizard

A **lizard** is a small reptile. The **lizard** lay on the rock in the hot sun.

M

mammals

A **mammal** is a warm-blooded animal. Cats are **mammals**.

manatees

A **manatee** is a plant-eating animal with flippers and a flat tail that lives in warm water. When we visited Florida, we saw **manatees** swimming in the water.

O

ocean

An **ocean** is a large body of salt water. It's fun to sail on the **ocean**.

P

paint

To **paint** means to cover something with color. Aunt Carly likes to **paint** houses.

penguins

A **penguin** is a kind of bird that lives in cold places. **Penguins** keep their chicks warm.

R

race

A **race** is a contest to find out who is the fastest. Selena got to the finish line first and won the **race**.

reptiles

A **reptile** is a cold-blooded animal. Snakes are **reptiles**.

roadrunner

A **roadrunner** is a very fast bird. We saw a **roadrunner** in the Arizona desert.

S

school

A **school** is a place where students learn from teachers. My best friend and I go to the same **school**.

sea otters

Sea otters are mammals with thick, brown fur that live in and by the ocean. After a swim, **sea otters** like to sit in the warm sun.

seeds
A **seed** is a part of a plant. Most plants grow from tiny little **seeds**.

snow
Snow is tiny pieces of frozen water that fall from the clouds. When we woke up, the ground was covered with **snow**.

snowman
A **snowman** looks like a person made of snow. We piled three balls of snow on top of each other and made a **snowman**.

spring
Spring is the season that comes after winter. In the **spring**, the flowers begin to bloom.

summer
Summer is the season that comes after spring. This **summer** my family will go to the beach.

T

tadpoles

A **tadpole** is a baby frog. I found **tadpoles** swimming in our pond.

tails

A **tail** is a part of some animals' bodies. Rats have long **tails**.

tall

To be **tall** is to stand high above the ground. The giraffe is very **tall**.

turtle

A **turtle** is a reptile with a shell. The **turtle** went inside its shell as soon as I touched it.

W

warm

Warm means not very hot. The tea was still **warm** after it sat for a while.

whales

A **whale** is the biggest mammal that lives in the ocean. When we went boating, we saw **whales** as big as our boat!

wings

A **wing** is a part that helps something to fly. The bird flapped its **wings** and flew away.

winter

Winter is a season that comes after fall. Last **winter** was very cold!

Z

zebra

A **zebra** is a striped animal that looks like a horse. My favorite animal is the **zebra**.

Credits

Placement Key:
(r) right, (l) left, (c) center, (t) top, (b) bottom, (bg) background

Photo Credits
3 (cl) ©Photodisc/Getty Images; **3** (tl) ©Houghton Mifflin Harcourt; **3** (b) ©Melba Photo Agency/Alamy Images; **5** (tl) ©J.A. Kraulis/Masterfile; **5** (bl) ©2007 Jupiterimages; **5** (br) ©2007 PunchStock; **6** (bl) © Steve Skjold / Alamy; **7** (tl) ©Bela Baliko Photography and Publishing Inc; **7** (bl) ©blickwinkel/McPhoto / Alamy; Blind [**9**] ©Design Pics Inc./David Ponton/Alamy Images; **10** (tr) ©Photodisc/Getty Images; **10** (br) ©Corbis; **10** (cl) ©Photodisc/Getty Images; **10** (tl) ©Houghton Mifflin Harcourt; **11** (tr) ©Corbis; **11** (tl) ©Amanda Friedman/Stone/Getty Images; **11** (cl) ©George Grall/National Geographic/Getty Images; **11** (cr) ©Stockbyte/Getty Images; **11** (bl) ©George Grall/National Geographic/Getty Images; **11** (br) ©Purestock/Getty Images; **12** © WaterFrame / Alamy; **14** ©Getty Images; **14** Courtesy of Rozanne Williams; **16** ©Brand X Pictures/Getty Images; **17** (c) Digital Vision/Getty Images; **18** David B Fleetham/Getty Images; **19** (tr) blickwinkel / Alamy; **20** (t) Science Source / Photo Researchers, Inc.; **20** Corbis; **21** (tr) Corbis; **22** Douglas Faulkner/Getty Images; **23** (tr) WaterFrame / Alamy; **24** Digital Vision/Getty Images; **25** (tr) M. Timothy O'Keefe / Alamy; **26** Mark Conlin / Alamy; **27** (tr) Mark Conlin / Alamy; **28** ©Houghton Mifflin Harcourt; **29** (tr) ©Melba Photo Agency/Alamy Images; **30** ©Houghton Mifflin Harcourt; **31** ©Photodisc/Alamy Images; **32** (tr) © Jake Hellbach / Alamy; **33** (c) Jose Luis Pelaez/Getty Images; **33** (tr) ©Houghton Mifflin Harcourt; **34** (inset) ©Lew Robertson/Getty Images; **34** (tl) ©Photodisc/Getty Images; **36** (bg) ©Photodisc/Getty Images; **36** ©Photodisc/Getty Images; **37** (cr) Photos.com/Jupiterimages/Getty Images; **37** (tr) ©Joel Simon/Digital Vision/Getty Images; **37** (tl) ©Houghton Mifflin Harcourt; **37** (tl) ©Photodisc/Getty Images; **42** (tl) © PhotoDisc/Getty Images; **42** (b) ©Alan D. Carey/Photodisc/Getty Images; **43** (tl) ©Design Pics Inc./Alamy; **43** (tr) ©Roger Tidman/CORBIS&#x0B;; **43** (bl) ©Gallo Images/Alamy; **43** (cl) ©Ann &

Steve Toon/Robert Harding World Imagery/Getty Images; **43** (bl) ©Rainer Jahns/Alamy; **43** (br) ©Tom Nebbia/Corbis; **44** Steve Bloom Images / Alamy; **45** (bg) **L12**: © Getty Images/Digital Vision; **65** ©stefanie van der vin/Fotolia; **67** Photodisc/Getty Images; **70** (bg) ©Tony Craddock/Photo Researchers, Inc.; **71** (cr) © Picture Partners / Alamy; **71** (br) ©Digital Vision/Getty Images; **73** ©Richard Hutchings/Photo Edit; **76** (t) ©Andrew Duke/Alamy; **76** (tl) ©J.A. Kraulis/Masterfile; **77** (tr) ©Jean Louis Bellurget/Stock Image/Jupiterimages; **77** (cl) ©Pete Turner/The Image Bank/Getty Images; **77** (bl) ©Ryan McVay/Taxi/Getty Images; **77** (bl) ©VEER Gildo Spadoni/Photonica/Getty Images; **77** (bl) ©Steve Mason/PhotoDisc/Getty Images; **78** ©HMH; **78** (tl) ©J.A. Kraulis/Masterfile; **80** ©J.A. Kraulis/Masterfile; **82** ©2007 Masterfile Corporation; **84** ©Bill Leaman/Dembinsky Photo; **85** ©Richard Hutchings/Photo Edit; **86** ©2007 Jupiterimages; **88** ©Masterfile; **89** ©2007 Masterfile Corporation; **90** ©2007 Masterfile Corporation; **92** (bg) ©Garry Black/Masterile; **93** (c) ©2007 PunchStock; **94** ©Tim Pannell/Corbis; **96** (c) ©George McCarthy/naturepl.com; **97** ©2007 PunchStock; **97** (t) ©BrandX; **98** (t) ©2007 PunchStock; **98** (bl) ©Richard Hutchings/Photo Edit; **99** (b) ©2007 PunchStock; **100** (tl) ©J.A. Kraulis/Masterfile; **101** ©Richard Hutchings/Photo Edit; **103** (tl) ©J.A. Kraulis/Masterfile; **103** (c) © willy matheisl/Alamy; **115** (br) © Cartesia/Photodisc/Getty Images; **115** (tl) ©J.A. Kraulis/Masterfile; **115** (cr) ©Jerzyworks/Masterfile; **120** (tc) © Steve Skjold / Alamy; **120** (t) ©ARCO/H Reinhard; **120** (b) © John Foxx/Stockbyte/Getty Images; **121** (tl) ©Danita Delimont/Alamy Images; **121** (tr) ©Photos.com; **121** (cl) ©Photos.com; **121** (cr) ©Jonathan Blair/Crocodile Fotos; **121** (bl) ©QT LUONG/Terra Galleria Photography; **121** (br) ©franzfoto.com/Alamy; **122** ©Alistair Berg/Getty Images; **145** (l) © PhotoAlto / Alamy; **145** (r) © PhotoAlto / Alamy; **148** (r) Big Cheese Photo LLC / Alamy; **148** (tl) © Steve Skjold / Alamy; **149** (tl) Steve Skjold / Alamy; **149** (r) Jose Luis Pelaez/Getty Images; **149** (b) Patrick LaCroix / Alamy; **150** Arctic-Images / Alamy; **151** (b) Jim West / Alamy; **151** (t) Ron Chapple Stock / Alamy; **152** (t) Superstudio/Getty Images; **152** (bg) imagebroker / Alamy; **153** (t) © Visions of America, LLC /